CHARITIES IN ACTION

FIGHTING
POVERTY

Nicola Barber

www.raintreepublishers.co.uk
Visit our website to find out
more information about
Raintree books.

To order:
☎ Phone 0845 6044371
🗎 Fax +44 (0) 1865 312263
💻 Email myorders@raintreepublishers.co.uk

Customers from outside the UK please telephone +44 1865 312262

Raintree is an imprint of Capstone Global Library
Limited, a company incorporated in England and
Wales having its registered office at 7 Pilgrim Street,
London, EC4V 6LB – Registered company number:
6695582

Text © Capstone Global Library Limited 2012
First published in hardback in 2012
Paperback edition first published in 2013
The moral rights of the proprietor have been
asserted.

Edited by Andrew Farrow, Adam Miller, and
  Diyan Leake
Designed by Victoria Allen
Picture research by Ruth Blair
Illustrations by Oxford Designers & Illustrators
Originated by Capstone Global Library Ltd
Printed and bound in China by Leo Paper
  Products Ltd

ISBN 978 1 406 23845 7 (hardback)
16 15 14 13 12
10 9 8 7 6 5 4 3 2 1

ISBN 978 1 406 23852 5 (paperback)
17 16 15 14 13
10 9 8 7 6 5 4 3 2 1

British Library Cataloguing in Publication Data
Barber, Nicola.
Fighting poverty. -- (Charities in action)
362.5'57632-dc23
A full catalogue record for this book is available from
the British Library.

Acknowledgements
The author and publisher are grateful to the
following for permission to reproduce copyright
material: Alamy pp. 13 (© Stuart Walker), 23 (© Picture
Contact BV), 33 (© Penny Tweedie), 35 (© Robert
Harding Picture Library Ltd), 37 (© Adrian Arbib),
51 (© Joerg Boethling), 53 (© Richard Human;
Corbis pp. 11 (© Gideon Mendel for Action Aid),
15 (© Thierry Gouegnon/Reuters), 16 (© Fred
Prouser/Reuters), 31 (© Punit Paranjpe/Reuters), 39
(© Reuters), 45 (© Karen Kasmauski/Science Faction),
48 (© Warren Toda/epa), 55 (© Adi Weda/epa; Getty
Images pp. 43 (Tony Karumba/AFP), 47 (Laureus), 57
(Peter Macdiarmid); PA Photos p. 25 (AP); Shutterstock
pp. 27 (© Lisa F. Young), 29 (© Zoran Karapancev),
41 (© Space Factory); © SOS Children pp. 19, 21;
© Venkatraman Memorial Trust pp. 5, 7.

Cover photograph of survivors carrying relief goods
in a tsunami-devastated village in Indonesia, 31
October 2010, reproduced with permission of Corbis
(© Mast Irham/epa).

Every effort has been made to contact copyright
holders of material reproduced in this book. Any
omissions will be rectified in subsequent printings if
notice is given to the publisher.

CONTENTS

Words printed in **bold** are explained in the glossary.

A WAY OUT OF POVERTY

The story begins with a chance meeting on a beach on the beautiful Coromandel coast in Tamil Nadu, south-east India. An English woman called Sylvia Holder was visiting the coast, staying in a hotel near the village of Kovalam. One day, she decided to walk along the beach towards the village. She came across a boy who told her that his name was Venkat, and that he was 12 years old.

The two started talking. Venkat came from a poor family. In fact, as Sylvia was to find out, Kovalam is a community of poor families who rely almost entirely on fishing to eke out a livelihood. Venkat told her that he wanted to continue going to school, but that his family could not afford the fees. Could Sylvia give him £10, he asked?

On the spur of the moment, Sylvia agreed not only to give Venkat the £10 to cover the school fees for one year, but also to carry on paying for his education. Over the following years, she kept in close touch with Venkat and his family. Venkat worked hard at school, graduated from Madras (Chennai) University, and went on to set up his own business.

The Venkatraman Memorial Trust

Then, in December 2003, at the age of 27, Venkat was killed in a road accident. Determined to make something positive out of this tragedy, Sylvia decided to set up the Venkatraman Memorial Trust. In 2004, she returned to Kovalam to find out how best to help the village. A visit to the local primary school quickly gave her an answer. It was overcrowded – many children were taught outside in the hot sun because of lack of classroom space. There were too few staff and there was very little equipment. So, in memory of Venkat, the Trust focused its efforts on improving the school for the benefit of all the children of Kovalam.

While Sylvia continues to run the Trust in the United Kingdom, Venkat's elder brother, Janakiraman, and his close friend M. Ali, oversee all the projects in Kovalam itself.

From small beginnings...

Since 2004, the Venkatraman Memorial Trust has bought equipment including computers and sewing machines; provided uniforms; employed teachers; built classrooms, a dining hall and sports facilities; and paid for an annual excursion for the children. It has also sponsored poor children from Kovalam through school and on to university. Its latest and most ambitious project is the construction of a brand-new high school where 1,000 pupils from Kovalam and surrounding villages will be able to study.

One of the charity's attractions for many of its supporters is that every single penny donated goes directly to Kovalam – Sylvia and her fellow trustees pay for any expenses in the United Kingdom. This small charity has a narrow focus, unlike many of the much larger charities discussed in this book. But the money raised has made a real difference to the lives and futures of the children of Kovalam, as we shall see on the next pages.

Sylvia Holder in Kovalam with some of the children she has helped through her charity, the Venkatraman Memorial Trust.

Sumithra's story

On Boxing Day 2004, a tsunami, caused by a massive undersea earthquake, devastated communities all around the Indian Ocean. The tsunami killed thousands of people in India, mainly along the south-eastern coast.

In Kovalam, the villagers saw the huge wave rolling in and many were able to escape. The wave pounded houses into rubble and threw the wooden fishing boats around. Sadly, in the chaos, ten people died.

One of the dead was the father of Sumithra and Kali. Here, Sumithra describes the life of the family before the tsunami, and the events of that terrible day:

> When I was a child, my parents, brother, and I lived in a small, dilapidated palm leaf house with no electricity and the roof was full of holes. The rain would come in during the monsoon and so would the snakes, from the tree next to our house, which made me very scared...

> When I was 12, the tsunami struck. My father, who was a fisherman, was on the beach mending his nets and he was hit by a boat flying through the air. He was critically injured and he died a few days later. It was a terrible and very sad time for us. My father had been the only breadwinner in the family so as well as coping with our grief, we were even poorer than before.

The newly formed Venkatraman Memorial Trust stepped in to help Sumithra and Kali. They were the first two children to receive **sponsorship** from the Trust to allow them to go to school. A separate appeal, set up by the Trust to raise money for victims of the tsunami in Kovalam, also paid for a new brick house for the family.

Thanks to continuing sponsorship from the Trust, Sumithra is studying computer science at Madras (Chennai) University. After graduating, she expects to be able to get a good job in Chennai, which is a major IT centre.

The benefits of sponsorship

Sumithra describes her life now and hopes for the future:

"Since my father died, my mother has been working long hours as a cleaner. We have breakfast together before she leaves the house at 7.30 a.m. – the leftovers from the night before – and I buy rice cakes for my lunch when I'm at college which cost 5 rupees (7p). My mother buys fish and vegetables for us to eat for dinner and I do the cooking for the family when I get back from college.

As my mother earns only 80 rupees a day (just over £1), the sponsorship money makes a huge difference to us and we are happy to know that Kali and I now have the prospect of earning good money when we are qualified. We will then be able to look after our mother and afford a much better lifestyle when we marry and have our own children. I just wish my father had lived to see me go to university – he would have been so proud."

Both Sumithra and her brother Kali have benefited from long-term help from the Venkatraman Memorial Trust.

What is poverty?

Look up the word *poverty* in a dictionary, and you will most likely find a definition based around a lack of "money or material possessions". People who do not have an adequate income to meet basic needs – food, shelter, health care, and education – are said to be poor. The amount required for people to have a minimum standard of living is often defined as the "**poverty line**" or "poverty threshold", and this amount varies hugely from country to country. In a **more economically developed country (MEDC)** such as the United States, for example, the minimum needed for a single person to survive (the poverty threshold) in 2011 was calculated at $10,830 (£6,920) per year – roughly $30 (£19) per day. But in a **less economically developed country (LEDC)** such as Bangladesh, $30 (£19) per day would easily buy all of a person's daily needs. In fact, the average daily income in Bangladesh in 2009 was just $1.60 (£1) per day. According to the **World Bank**, 40 per cent of the population in Bangladesh were below the national poverty line in the same year.

LEDCs and MEDCs

These terms are used to describe differences in wealth between countries around the globe:

• Less economically developed countries (LEDCs) are the poorer countries of the world. They are mainly found in the southern hemisphere, and are mainly in the continents of Africa and Asia.

• More economically developed countries (MEDCs) are the richer countries of the world. They are mainly found in the northern hemisphere and include countries in North America, Europe, and Japan in Asia.

See page 58 for more information.

International measures

The huge differences between LEDCs and MEDCs make it difficult to compare one country directly with another. For this reason, global organizations such as the United Nations and the World Bank have developed international measures of poverty. In 2008, the World Bank established a world poverty line of $1.25 (80p) per day. Using this measure, it showed that the number of people in LEDCs living below the poverty line fell from 1.8 billion (1,800 million) in 1990 to under 1.4 billion in 2005. However, the majority of this reduction took place in China. According to World Bank figures, 37 per cent of the world's poor were found in China in 1990. By 2005, this number had declined to 15 per cent. Meanwhile, the number of people living in poverty in **sub-Saharan Africa** and South Asia actually increased during the same period.

This map is a guide to the locations mentioned throughout the book.

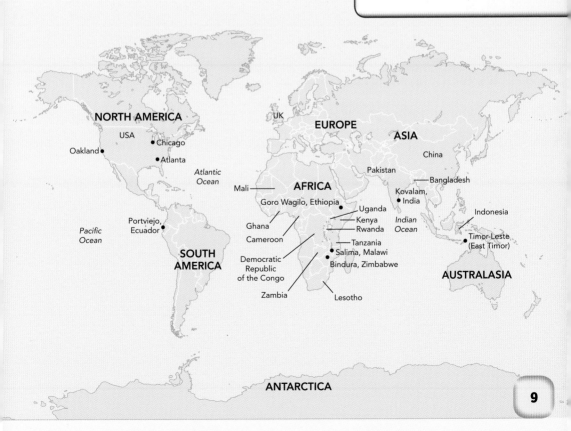

Absolute and relative poverty

For many people in LEDCs, the reality of living below the $1.25 poverty line is not having enough to eat, not having adequate shelter or clothing, and not having access to health care or education. This is known as **absolute poverty**. Yet poverty is not confined to the poorer regions of the world. If you live in an MEDC, where the majority of people own a television, a computer, or a car, then you may consider yourself to be poor if you cannot afford such things. In fact, not being able to afford a computer or a car may affect your ability to get a job or to complete your education. This is known as **relative poverty**.

UN Millennium Development Goals

In 2000, 189 countries worldwide signed up to the United Nations' Millennium Declaration. This document sets out eight **Millennium Development Goals (MDGs)** with the target of meeting them by 2015. The aim of the MDGs is to tackle poverty and its related issues by:

- eradicating (ending) extreme poverty and hunger
- ensuring all children are able to complete a full course of primary schooling
- promoting **gender equality** (equality between men and women) and giving women more control over their lives
- reducing the number of deaths of children under five
- improving mothers' health
- combating **HIV/AIDS**, malaria, and other diseases
- ensuring a **sustainable** environment
- developing a partnership between countries worldwide.

Expanding the definition

While income is an important measurement of poverty, the definition of poverty is often expanded to take into account quality of life. The Indian economist and **Nobel Prize** winner, Amartya Sen, has pioneered this way of thinking about poverty. He links poverty to "capability" rather than simply the lowness of income. Some of the basic capabilities defined by Sen include living to old age, living in safety and health, as well as being treated as a dignified human being whose worth is equal to that of others. Sen's work has helped to link poverty with a wide range of issues including hunger, health care, education, political rights, gender, and inequality. All of these issues are addressed by the wide range of charities discussed in this book.

UN *definition of poverty*

The United Nations' 1998 definition of poverty reflects the broad-based approach pioneered by Amartya Sen:

"Fundamentally, poverty is a denial of choices and opportunities, a violation of human dignity. It means lack of basic capacity to participate effectively in society. It means not having enough to feed and cloth[e] a family, not having a school or clinic to go to, not having the land on which to grow one's food or a job to earn one's living, not having access to **credit**. *It means insecurity, powerlessness and exclusion of individuals, households and communities. It means susceptibility to violence, and it often implies living on marginal or fragile environments, without access to clean water or* **sanitation**.*"*

These women are washing their clothes and collecting water from a hand pump at a relief camp in Pakistan after devastating flooding forced them to flee their homes in 2010.

THE FIGHT AGAINST POVERTY

Many of the charities in this book started when a person, or group of people, felt strongly enough about one person, one issue, or one country, to try to make a difference. Some of the charities have chosen to stay small and focused on a specific area (for example, the Venkatraman Memorial Trust – see pages 4–5). Others, such as Oxfam, have developed and grown to become global household names. This chapter examines some of these charities, and their fight against poverty.

Oxfam

Oxfam started in the United Kingdom during World War II, in response to a crisis in Greece, where people were dying from starvation. After the end of the war, Oxfam continued to help victims of war as well as the poor and hungry.

As Oxfam expanded throughout the 1960s and 1970s, its focus changed from the immediate relief of suffering to working together with poor communities. The charity employed local representatives in LEDCs to run projects that enabled people to improve their own lives.

This principle of community involvement and working closely with local groups remains very important in Oxfam's work (see the case study on pages 14–15). In the 21st century, Oxfam is a truly global charity, with 15 organizations around the world operating under the Oxfam name.

Achieving dignity for all

"Every job at Oxfam is a responsible one – whatever your role, its ultimate goal will be to help every person on this planet towards a life of dignity and opportunity."

Barbara Stocking, Director of Oxfam GB

Working for Oxfam

What is it like to work for a large charity such as Oxfam? You certainly need a strong belief in what the charity stands for – that poverty and suffering are injustices that you can help to overcome by working for Oxfam. You also need to enjoy working alongside a wide range of people who may come from very different cultural and language backgrounds from yours. You need to be flexible and adaptable and able to work efficiently and cost-effectively – remembering always that Oxfam raises all its revenue from hard-earned donations. One advantage of working for a large organization is the variety of jobs on offer, and the opportunities you may have within the charity.

Depending on their qualifications and experience, people can apply to Oxfam to work in a wide range of roles including fundraiser, campaigner, administrator, project officer, and **humanitarian** worker. Some jobs are based in a particular country or region, while others involve a lot of travel internationally.

Oxfam charity shops are a common sight in the towns and cities of the United Kingdom.

Oxfam in Ghana

This case study is an example of a large charity that is able to work on a large scale. Oxfam has been active in the West African country of Ghana since 1986. For many years, Oxfam helped families in poverty by providing basic services such as water and sanitation, education, and health care.

Ghana suffers from a north–south divide, with people in the northern regions of the country being considerably poorer than in the south. The north is mainly savannah (grassland), while the south is covered with rainforest that has been cleared in places to plant crops such as cocoa, pineapples, and mangoes. Agriculture is a very important part of the Ghanaian economy, accounting for about half of all employment.

Partnerships

Ghana is expected to meet the first MDG (see page 10) by 2015. The number of people living below the international poverty line almost halved between 1991 and 2005, from 52 per cent to 28 per cent of the population.

This improvement has been experienced mostly in the south of the country, where **cash crops** such as cocoa are grown, and people have benefited from increased income. In parts of the north, poverty is actually on the increase. In these regions, people often struggle to grow enough crops for food, and there has been little investment in cash crops such as the shea nuts that grow there.

Since 2009, Oxfam has changed the emphasis of its work in Ghana. Instead of projects to help farmers directly, Oxfam is focusing on helping farmers to have a say in important decisions that shape their futures. This work is known as **advocacy** – helping people to organize and campaign, and to have a voice.

To do this, Oxfam is working in partnership with other charities and **non-governmental organizations (NGOs)**, some based in Ghana itself, and some from other countries around the world. The aim is for small farmers, particularly from the north, to have a greater say in the political policies that affect them.

Giving power to the poor

"When poor people have clout in the market, the community and the family, and those who hold power are obliged to listen and respond, real improvements in people's lives can occur."

From Poverty to Power, Oxfam International, 2008

A woman sells blocks of shea butter at a street market in the Ivory Coast. Shea butter is used in many cosmetic products, as well as for cooking.

Shea butter

Shea butter comes from nuts that grow across the northern regions of Ghana. The kernel (inside) of the nut is processed by hand, usually by women, to turn it into shea butter, a soft white paste. Shea butter can be used in food products, cosmetics, and pharmaceutical products (medicines). It has great value on the international market and it provides important income for communities in northern Ghana. Yet it has received very little attention compared to the cash crops grown in the south. Oxfam has joined forces with local organizations, as well as NGOs, to establish a network of shea producers. Working together, the shea farmers will have more power to influence policies and improve their lives.

Celebrities and charities

Charities use a wide variety of different strategies to encourage people from MEDCs to become involved in their work. Many are happy to make use of the power of celebrity. Famous people such as actors, sports personalities, or musicians are often willing to use their fame to help make people more aware of a particular cause. This type of approach definitely works best when the celebrity is seen to be interested in and knowledgeable about the cause he or she is supporting.

In the United States, for example, Save the Children has Artist Ambassadors – well-known actors and musicians who are prepared to "lend their names, faces and personal interests to various Save the Children programmes about which they feel particularly passionate". One of these ambassadors is the actor America Ferrera, star of *Ugly Betty*. In 2010, she travelled to Mali on behalf of Save the Children. Using short films about her trip uploaded to You Tube and a Facebook page, America brings to life the charity's work to improve education in this poor country. As she says in one of the films: "These really are the places that need assistance, these really are the children and villages that need us to find them…"

America Ferrera arrives at the premiere for the film *Enchanted* in Hollywood. As an internationally recognized actor, she also works as an Artist Ambassador for Save the Children.

America Ferrera, Artist Ambassador

"I can't imagine anyone who would come and would see and then would think there isn't any way for them to help."

America Ferrera, on her trip to Mali, one of the poorest countries in the world

Sponsoring a child

Another strategy used by some charities is to link those giving money and those receiving it by setting up sponsorship schemes. **Donors** agree to give a certain amount of money on a regular basis, and in return they receive information about their sponsored child, and his or her progress. Some donors write and send gifts, and some even make a visit to meet their sponsored child. Charities that set up these schemes include Plan International, World Vision, ActionAid, and SOS Children.

Sponsoring

You can find out more about charities that run sponsorship schemes:

- Plan International: plan-international.org. Plan works to promote children's rights and to lift them out of poverty.
- World Vision: www.worldvision.org.uk. World Vision focuses on reducing the effects of poverty on children.
- ActionAid: www.actionaid.org.uk. ActionAid improves people's lives and works towards changing the situation that keeps people poor.
- SOS Children: www.soschildrensvillages.org.uk. SOS Children provides homes for orphaned and abandoned children in Children's Villages around the world.

Using sponsorship money

All of these charities spend the money raised through sponsorship in different ways. Although donors to Plan International and World Vision sponsor individual children, the money given to both charities is collected together and used for projects that will benefit whole communities in the sponsored child's country.

SOS Children focuses its work on orphaned and abandoned children. As its website states, SOS Children "looks after children whose parents are not there to care for them and have no one else to care for them". The charity provides a home, a family, and a "mother" for these children in purpose-built communities called Children's Villages. The money provided by donors goes directly to the specific community in which the sponsored child lives. (You can read more about SOS Children's Villages on pages 19–21.)

Sponsorship schemes pros and cons

Pros

• Sponsorship schemes provide a regular source of income so charities can plan for the long term.
• Donors feel connected to their sponsored child and take an interest in their welfare.
• These charities provide care for some of the poorest and most vulnerable children.

Cons

• Keeping each individual donor informed about his or her sponsored child is time-consuming and costly.
• Some donors do not regularly write or send gifts to their sponsored children – this can make children feel unhappy and left out.
• Some donors may be unhappy that the money they are giving is not going directly to their sponsored child.

SOS Children's Villages

SOS Children's Villages care for orphaned and abandoned children in 124 countries around the world, including the United States and several European countries. The children are given the comfort and security of a home in a village, a family of up to 10 children, and a "mother". They can stay in this home until they are old enough to live independent lives. The charity also supports the poorest families who cannot afford to look after their own children. Rather than split up families by taking the children away, the charity's Family Strengthening Programmes help people in poverty with support such as food parcels, paying for school fees, and providing training for work.

Edward's story

Edward lives with his two younger brothers in Zimbabwe. In 2007, the family was devastated when both the boys' parents died from HIV/AIDS. Ten-year-old Edward was left to look after his brothers. He was unable to go to school, and he struggled to find enough money to feed his family. Luckily, in 2008 the three boys were sent to SOS Children's Village Bindura. "I'm very happy to be in a home with my two brothers and SOS family members – I'm happy to be back at school after so long!" Edward says.

Edward's story is not unusual in Zimbabwe. Many families have been affected by the rapid spread of HIV/AIDS in Africa, and children are often left without parents to look after them. SOS Children's Village Bindura provides a home for up to 180 children, many of whom are HIV/AIDS orphans.

SOS mothers

There are more than 5,000 SOS mothers in Children's Villages across the world. They are on the front line of the charity's work. The mothers live with the children, care for them every day and, in cases when a mother can no longer care for her child, often take over the role of a child's natural mother. SOS mothers complete two years' basic training before starting work. This training covers areas such as **nutrition**, child development, and **counselling**. Many of the children that come into their care have had traumatic experiences before reaching the safety of an SOS Children's Village. All SOS mothers learn how to support these children to overcome their difficult starts in life.

Zoila, SOS mother

"I am proud of being a mother, and I feel happy to have the chance to care for innocent, ingenious, and mischievous creatures: my sons and daughters ... I don't have children myself, but these kids really make me feel like a mother: more human, fuller of life. This work is hard, but the recompense of my children is absolutely great."

Zoila, an SOS mother in Portoviejo, Ecuador

Behind the scenes in the UK

As a charity, SOS Children prides itself on spending its money wisely, and particularly on keeping its fundraising and administrative costs as low as possible. In 2010, the charity's income was over £9 million ($14 million). Around 40 per cent of this income came from the regular payments paid by individual sponsors, which provide the backbone of the charity's long-term funding. Another 20 per cent came from companies and large donations; 25 per cent was raised from charity events, school donations, and money left in wills. The final 15 per cent came from educational trusts and HSBC Bank.

The charity's main method of communicating with donors, and with the wider public, is on the internet – through its website and online advertising. The Chief Executive of SOS Children, Andrew Cates, writes that the charity manages to achieve fantastic results without "junk mail, doorstep fundraising, cold telephone calling, TV or print adverts or indeed spam ... People surf our website when they are ready and interested to read about our work ... Other aspects of the story include having very good projects to sell, having very good fundraising staff to follow up interest and also having very good quality volunteers."

SOS Children's fundraisers

The charity has 20 full- and part-time employees in its UK offices. Its fundraising roles include working with:

- companies
- community groups
- individual donors
- university support groups
- schools

The fundraising director manages these employees. There is also a team of people who look after the website and the charity's online activity. You can find out more about this charity at: www.soschildrensvillages.org.uk.

This Sri Lankan family's home was rebuilt by SOS Children.

POVERTY AT HOME

Most people reading this book are likely to live in a more economically developed country. They are unlikely to suffer from the extremes of absolute poverty (see page 10) experienced in the poorest countries of the world. But relative poverty is a real issue for many households in the wealthier countries.

Income poverty in the UK

In the United Kingdom, the government produces national statistics for households in income poverty – where income falls below 60 per cent of the average (median) United Kingdom income. The figures for 2010 showed that 3.8 million children (29 per cent) and 7.9 million working-age adults (22 per cent) lived in income poverty in the United Kingdom.

The cycle of poverty

UK-based charities, such as the Joseph Rowntree Foundation and the Child Poverty Action Group, link poverty strongly to children's ability to do well in life – as does the US National Center for Children in Poverty. For example, children from poor families are more likely to have health problems and are less likely to do well at school.

Without adequate qualifications, these children are also less likely to go on to find good jobs and be able to lift themselves out of poverty in the future. This is known as the cycle of poverty.

What does poverty mean in MEDCs?

Professor Peter Townsend, a social scientist and leading campaigner for justice for the poor, devised a definition of poverty that is widely used in MEDCs:

> Individuals, families, and groups in the population can be said to be in poverty when they lack the resources to obtain the types of diet, participate in the activities, and have the living conditions and amenities which are customary, or are at least widely encouraged and approved, in the societies in which they belong.

Welfare and charities

Most MEDCs have welfare systems to assist people who cannot afford the basics of life, such as housing, food, or other necessities. But even with these safeguards, charities have an important role to play in ensuring that the poorest people have shelter at night, food to eat, and access to basic health care. For example, the case study on pages 24–26 illustrates the number of people in the US city of Chicago who rely on food rescue organizations to be able to survive from day to day.

A girl stands on the balcony of her flat in a town in Bulgaria. Many children in Europe live in relative poverty compared to the national average.

Greater Chicago Food Depository

The United States is one of the wealthiest countries in the world. Yet millions of Americans cannot afford to feed their families. According to a study carried out in 2010 by Feeding America, 37 million Americans, including 14 million children, rely on food banks and food rescue organizations for their weekly food supplies. Even in families where one parent is working, people are having to choose between paying for food and other basic essentials such as housing, electricity, and medical care.

The Greater Chicago Food Depository is the main hub for charitable food distribution across the whole of Cook County, Illinois. The food arrives at its large warehouse from food retailers and manufacturers – food that might otherwise have gone to waste. Local communities also run "food drives" to encourage people to donate food to the Depository. All the donated food is inspected, sorted, and repacked by volunteers and employees at the warehouse before being sent out for distribution. The food goes out to 650 food pantries, soup kitchens, and shelters around the county. These are the places where people come to pick up food or to have a meal and a chat. They are all staffed by volunteers.

What's it like to be a volunteer?

There are many different jobs to do. Some volunteers cook and serve meals, then help to clean up afterwards. Others use their muscle power to fetch and carry groceries, particularly for elderly people who cannot manage on their own. Sometimes, the work might be a bit boring – stocking shelves maybe, or checking lists. But it is fun to work as part of a team, and as one volunteer puts it: "It feels good to help people who need help."

Help the hungry

"Everybody deserves food. Those who have should help those who have not. How can a child concentrate in school if he is hungry? This is a humbling experience."
LaVerne Morris, Director, St Columbanus Food Pantry

Community Kitchens

As well as providing much-needed food, the Food Depository uses its resources in other ways to try to help people out of poverty. Unemployed adults who want to work in the food industry can become students in one of the Community Kitchens. The programme is free. During their 14-week training, students learn many of the skills they would need for work in a professional kitchen. The students prepare meals that are delivered to children and elderly people all over Cook County.

A life change

"I was nervous about a change in my life. This has been a big step in becoming more responsible."
Ricco Spencer, student at Chicago's Community Kitchens

Thanksgiving dinner turkeys provided by the Greater Chicago Food Depository are handed out to residents outside a church.

25

Advocacy

The mission of the Food Depository is "providing food for hungry people while striving to end hunger in our community". The campaigning part of the Food Depository's work is very important for the future. Volunteers can play their part by contacting their elected representatives to let them know that they support hunger-relief programmes. This type of work is called advocacy.

The St Columbanus Food Pantry, Chicago

The St Columbanus Food Pantry is part of the Greater Chicago Food Depository. The pantry opens at 10 a.m. every morning. However, rain or shine, the queue for food starts to form many hours before. In the words of Father Matthew Eyerman, pastor of St Columbanus Church, "Having to get in line at 6 a.m. for food, now that's a bad day. So, we try to get them through as fast as possible. You have to respect people, respect their time."

The pantry distributes food to roughly 500 people every week. Many come from working families, but they cannot make ends meet. The director of the pantry, LaVerne Morris says: "It's getting worse and worse ... They're working families, seniors. Park Manor [the area of Chicago served by the pantry] is the labor force of America. It's the working class. They never thought they'd be standing in line for food. But, taxes, utilities, medicine ... At least one person in every household we serve is working. I watch my neighbors come through this line. Don't they deserve to eat?"

A real need

Recently, some of the volunteers working at the pantry were students from Tanzania. "They [the students] are aghast, shocked that people have to stand in line for food in America," Father Eyerman says. The need is very real, however. While some volunteers serve people in the pantry, others load up a van with groceries for local residents who cannot manage the walk to the pantry. These elderly people rely on their weekly food parcel from the pantry.

The haves and the have-nots

Although many charities focus on providing the basic necessities such as shelter or food, there are others that exist to help people with other needs. A child who lives in a family that struggles to afford the week's rent and food bills is unlikely to have access to a wide range of books, or a computer. In a society where the ability to read, write, and use the internet is normal and vital, this child is deprived. In the United Kingdom, a charity called the e-Learning Foundation was set up in 2001 to bridge this "**digital divide**". Its aim is to ensure that every child has access to a computer at school and at home. It works with schools and parents to provide computers for their children, and to ensure that the funding is available long-term to replace and update equipment.

A computer is no luxury

"My charity, the e-Learning Foundation, helps disadvantaged children get access to a computer and the internet. A luxury? Not if richer kids are gaining a huge advantage by having good access. Poverty at its simplest is the nature of the gap between the haves and the have-nots."
Valerie Thompson, Chief Executive of the e-Learning Foundation

Having access to a computer is essential for children's future development.

A helping hand

Many charities focus on helping people to help themselves out of poverty. This type of work is very wide-ranging – some people need to study to gain more qualifications, some want to train for a particular job, and some need help to find their first job or set up a business. Charities that offer a helping hand can play a real part in transforming people's lives.

Goodwill Industries International

In the United States, Goodwill Industries International is a large organization made up of over 180 community-based groups. It provides job training and other programmes for people who are at a disadvantage in society – for example, those who lack qualifications, have been in prison, or have recovered from drug or alcohol addiction. Goodwill is funded by a network of charity shops as well as an online auction site. Its vision is that: "Every person has the opportunity to achieve his/her fullest potential and participate in and contribute to all aspects of life."

Goodwill works on a massive scale. In 2010, it helped more than 2.4 million people by funding employment and training programmes. Each one of these people has their own individual story to tell. Steve Jones is one of them.

Steve worked in a variety of low-paid jobs but could not make enough money to look after his family. One day, he went to the library and saw an advertisement for training in construction with the local Goodwill Industries centre. Steve decided to sign up. He is now on the training programme, but with his new skills and confidence he has also got a job as a sales manager.

Steve's new career

"Goodwill has given me the opportunity for a career, a job that I like and can grow with, and the joy of taking care of my children, as well as my responsibilities as a citizen..."

Steve Jones

All over the world, people take part in events such as marathons to raise huge amounts of money for charity.

Fundraising

All of the charities discussed in this book need funds to operate. They rely on the fact that many people are willing to give money to help others. Some people give one-off donations, while others donate small amounts regularly. Some leave instructions in their will for money to go to specific charities after their deaths. But charities also use a vast array of other money-making activities. Sporting challenges offer people the chance to have fun, get fit, and raise money all at the same time. Marathon running, triathlon, cycling, skydiving, and trekking are all popular. In schools, fun events include cake sales, dress-down days, dances, concerts, and talent competitions as well as sponsored events (such as swimming, running, spelling, or silence). The internet is also a powerful tool for fundraising. Some websites allow people to donate money every time they make a purchase from a particular online shop. Other sites, such as Justgiving, make it easy to raise sponsorship money by enabling people to donate online.

ENOUGH TO EAT?

An economist explains hunger

"Starvation is the characteristic of some people not having enough food to eat. It is not the characteristic of there being not enough food to eat."

Amartya Sen

Poverty is the problem

"... there is plenty of food in the world for everyone. The problem is that hungry people are trapped in severe poverty. They lack the money to buy enough food to nourish themselves. Being constantly malnourished, they become weaker and often sick. This makes them increasingly less able to work, which then makes them even poorer and hungrier..."

The anti-poverty website, www.poverty.com

The quotations in the boxes tell the story of hunger in the 21st century. There is no lack of food in the world. Yet there is massive inequality around the globe between those who have access to food and those who do not. In some places, natural disasters such as drought or earthquake mean that there is a genuine, short-term shortage of food. In these cases, charities and NGOs spring into action with urgent appeals for food aid to try to prevent people from dying of starvation. But in this chapter, we will examine the work of charities that are helping people in poverty who struggle in the long-term to provide enough food for themselves and their families.

Hunger facts

• Sixty-six per cent of all the hungry people in the world live in just seven countries: Bangladesh, China, the Democratic Republic of the Congo, Ethiopia, India, Indonesia, and Pakistan.

• The region with the highest proportion of hungry people is sub-Saharan Africa (the region that lies south of the Sahara Desert), where 30 per cent of the population lacked access to adequate food in 2010.

Working with farmers

Investment in agriculture plays a vital part in lifting people out of hunger and poverty. Most of the world's poorest people are small farmers who produce their own food. Helping these farmers to grow better crops more efficiently and sustainably is the aim of many charities around the world. Sometimes, projects are extremely simple – providing money for resources such as seeds and tools, for example. Sometimes they are more complicated – for example, investing in projects such as **terracing**, **irrigation** (supplying water), or storage systems.

There are as many different approaches to this work as there are different charities. For example, War on Want works in many countries with local campaigning organizations to ensure the voices and opinions of poor farmers are heard, while FarmAfrica provides direct support for rural farmers in Africa. The case studies on the following pages provide insights into another two charities that work with farmers in Africa.

An Indian rescue worker distributes food to survivors of the massive tsunami that devastated communities all around the Indian Ocean in December 2005. Such natural disasters require immediate aid to help those affected.

Send a Cow

In the 1980s, the **European Union** introduced quotas to limit the amount of milk produced in its member countries. Some dairy farmers in the United Kingdom found that they were being forced to slaughter healthy cows just to avoid being fined for producing too much milk. At the same time, Uganda in Africa was emerging from a time of civil war, large areas of farmland had been destroyed, and many people were struggling to feed themselves and their families.

A group of farmers in the United Kingdom decided to take action. They flew to Uganda, met with local farmers, and saw how they could help both in the short and long term. The idea was to send cows from the United Kingdom to Africa. In the short term, one cow provided milk to feed a family. In the longer term, the cow's manure was ideal for **fertilizing** the soil, allowing people to start growing crops again. This is how the charity Send a Cow was born.

Today, Send a Cow no longer sends live animals from Europe to Africa because a ban on importing live animals was introduced in 1996. It also makes more economic sense to source animals in the country to support local markets. Send a Cow continues to help poor families by providing suitable cows, sheep, goats, and pigs that are bought locally. It provides training and support and has widened its area of concern to include six other countries: Rwanda, Ethiopia, Lesotho, Kenya, Zambia, and Cameroon. The charity allows families to farm effectively and sustainably, and to work their way out of poverty for good.

The cow transforms our lives

Rwandan farmer Margaret Mukabasinga describes the difference Send a Cow has made:

> This cow is transforming our family life. She is providing milk for our children, which we could not afford before. We have a surplus to sell, which covers school expenses and family healthcare. Her manure fertilizes our garden, which yields enough vegetables to eat, share with neighbours, and sell ... This season, we expect good crops of bananas and beans – that will be a real life-changing opportunity.

Working for Send a Cow

Send a Cow has an office in the United Kingdom and experts based in sub-Saharan Africa. Farmers who have benefited from working with Send a Cow pass on their knowledge by training other farmers in their communities. Here are two examples:

Aklilu Dogisso is Country Director in Ethiopia. Before coming to Send a Cow in 2007, Aklilu worked for international NGOs such as World Vision. He says, "I love working for Send a Cow ... We help [poor families] open up their eyes to their potential and opportunities within their reach..."

Amsalu Haile lives in Bonke, one of the remotest areas of Ethiopia. Ten years ago, his children were hungry most of the time. With Send a Cow's help he started to grow food and became a successful farmer. Amsalu now passes on his knowledge – so far, he has trained 20 other farmers.

Eugenia Murebwaire was orphaned in the conflict in Rwanda. Send a Cow gave her goats to provide milk for herself and the other children she had to look after.

MERET is a joint venture between the Ethiopian government and the World Food Program (WFP). It helps people in poor communities who do not always have access to enough food to maintain active and healthy lives. Such people tend to be extremely vulnerable to changing circumstances around them, such as sudden rises in food prices or prolonged drought. MERET works with communities on projects that will give them food security, and help them to survive economic and environmental "shocks".

Food for work

MERET works by discussing with communities how best to address the problems they face on two fronts: improving the local environment and boosting local livelihoods. Once the programme has been decided, the local people carry out the necessary work over months, or sometimes years. These workers are paid in the form of food, which is funded and provided by WFP. "Food for work" gives people security while the programme is under way.

Goro Wagilo

In eastern Ethiopia, the people of Goro Wagilo village have seen rapid change over the past 15 years, thanks to a joint WFP/MERET programme. In the early 1990s, the outlook was grim for the village. People relied on wood as a fuel for cooking, and this had resulted in too many trees being cut down. The trees had protected the ground and their roots helped to hold the precious topsoil in place. Without the trees, the ground was bare and barren. Every time the rains fell, the water washed the soil away.

Tonkollu Letu and the other farmers of Goro Wagilo did not have the resources to tackle such a huge problem. Then in 1995, the community signed up to a MERET programme to reclaim their degraded land. The farmers spent eight years digging ditches, building dams, and constructing terraces along the hillsides. They were paid for their work in food.

Bare land

One of the farmers, Tonkollu Letu, described how the farmland looked: "It was like a man without clothes. The mountains were bare from deforestation [loss of forest]."

A success story

Today, rainwater no longer rushes down the bare slopes. Instead, the water is captured and held back by the terraces and in the irrigation channels. It can make its way slowly through the soil and feed the crops that grow on each terrace. Tonkollu and the other farmers of Goro Wagilo no longer need food aid. They can produce enough not only to feed themselves and their families, but also to sell at the local market. The extra money raised allows them to invest in their own future.

The story of Goro Wagilo was reported by one of the Public Information Officers working for the WFP. The job of gathering and preparing information about projects and events is vital to help the wider public understand the work of charities and NGOs.

These fertile fields in the countryside of Ethiopia show what can be achieved when farmers get support in managing their land.

Climate change

Global warming and **climate change** affect everyone on our planet. As our planet warms up, we are likely to experience:

- a rise in sea levels causing coastal flooding
- an increase in water shortages
- more extreme events such as droughts and floods.

Global warming is caused by emissions of carbon dioxide into the atmosphere. While it is the MEDCs that are responsible for most of these emissions, it is people living in poverty in the LEDCs who are most vulnerable to their effects. They are unlikely to have savings to fall back on in the event of an emergency such as drought. Also, many people live in makeshift homes on land that is prone to flooding or **landslide**.

Charities take the problems of climate change very seriously and are planning to try to reduce its impact on people in poverty. Many communities are already adapting to protect their livelihoods. The Deccan Development Society (DDS) is one example.

The Deccan Development Society

In India, the charity Christian Aid has had a long-term partnership with the DDS. It is active in southern India, in an area of the Deccan plateau that has hard, stony ground and little rain. It is difficult to make a living in the region, and the levels of poverty are high. However, the DDS has helped to transform agricultural methods in the region by working closely with groups of women farmers.

Owing to climate change, the already low rainfall has become even more erratic in recent history. To meet this challenge, the women farmers have moved away from crops such as rice and sugar cane, which require large amounts of water. Instead, they cultivate millet and sorghum, and a wide variety of other traditional crops. Farmer Gangwar Manemma explains the advantage of this approach:

> Every crop does something to the soil, while helping the other crops to grow, by way of providing safety against insects or enriching the soil with leaf fall. Further, we feel secure in the thought that if one crop fails, there is always one more to sustain us. Our animals too will have different kinds of fodder [foods]. These will keep them healthy and active. The best thing about this method is that our traditional crops are very hardy, and can survive under hostile conditions.

Global Cool

The aim of the UK-based charity Global Cool is to inspire people to think differently in order to live a greener lifestyle. It focuses on the areas where individual actions can have the biggest impact on carbon emissions – for example, energy use at home, driving, and flying. The charity uses the power of celebrities to promote simple ideas about saving the planet that are also fun – from wrapping up in stylish knitwear and turning down the heating, to encouraging flight-free holidays ("traincations").

A *fun approach*

"Unless all of us, in our daily lives, get our act together then we still won't crack it. I'm inspired by Global Cool's approach because planet saving has to be the thing which everyone wants to do. It's fun and rewarding and makes you feel good inside."

Tessa Tennant,
Trustee of Global Cool

A member of the Deccan Development Society in India examines seeds that have been collected and stored for food and reseeding.

37

Mercy Corps

Timor-Leste (East Timor) is one of Asia's newest and poorest countries. It achieved independence in 2002, but has suffered outbreaks of violence and unrest since then. The country is often affected by drought, but in 2010 it was torrential and unseasonal rains that caused a major problem. Timor-Leste's president, Ramos Horta, is aware that such unusual weather patterns are likely to occur more regularly as a result of climate change. In a speech at the United Nations, he warned of the dangers of climate change to people living on the edge of poverty.

An international charity

Mercy Corps is based in the United States, but is an international organization with offices all around the world. Dr Jim Jarvie is its Director of Climate Change, Environment and Natural Resource Management, with his main office in the United Kingdom. In 2010, he travelled to Timor-Leste and saw for himself the effects of the rain and floods. Driving into the remote south of the country, he noticed the poor state of the roads, made worse by the effect of the rains.

Dr Jarvie met a farmer called Donatus, who explained that in a typical year, his family and those of his neighbours would produce enough food to eat, and some surplus to sell. The money went on school fees for the children, health care, and a few luxuries. That year, the deluge had washed away paddy (rice) fields, and destroyed crops and houses; landslides swept away orchards. Owing to the torrential rains, there was no extra income.

A heart-warming welcome

"The charity and kindness that those in real need show to guests never ceases to amaze in this work, and our hosts in the fields, among their grass-thatched houses without power, clean water, or incomes was no exception."

Jim Jarvie on his visit to Timor-Leste in 2010

A reason for hope

Wahyu Nugroho is Mercy Corps'
Programme Manager in Timor-Leste.
He, too, has reported on the impact of
the rains in 2010. Travelling around the
country has become increasingly difficult
because the roads have been damaged.
Some roads are impassable, leaving
villages isolated.

But one visit gives Wahyu hope. A
blacksmith named Mario de Jesus has
received training from the UN Food and
Agriculture Organization to make metal
storage silos (containers). The water-
tight silos will help farmers to store food
for longer, and ensure that their families have a supply of
food. Wahyu wants to link Mario up with farmers supported by the
Mercy Corps programme, and Mario agrees. So next time the rains
come, it is possible that some of Timor-Leste's farmers will have
access to improved storage for their food.

Where does it go?

*Like all charities, Mercy
Corps gets its money
from fundraising and
donations. It spends
88 per cent of its income
on programmes such
as emergency response,
helping farmers, and small
business loans for women,
and 12 per cent of its
income on administration
and further fundraising.*

Members of the Mercy Corps move as quickly
as possible on programmes ranging from
bringing in food and supplies to enabling
people to rebuild their economy.

INEQUALITY

There are many different aspects of inequality. Poverty is often calculated by using averages, but these calculations do not tell the whole story. In many countries, average income measurements hide the huge inequalities between the rich and the poor. This type of inequality is found both in MEDCs and LEDCs.

In the United States, for example, the top-earning 10 per cent of households controlled more than 70 per cent of the country's wealth in 2007, while the 10 per cent of lowest earners controlled just 4 per cent. In South America, Brazil is one of the world's major emerging economies. Yet despite successful government schemes to lift millions of people out of poverty, it still has one of the biggest inequalities between rich and poor in the world.

It is also common to find other types of inequality within a society – for example, between people who live in rural and urban areas, or among minority groups. However, the inequality that many charities are focusing on worldwide is that of gender. This is because more than two-thirds (70 per cent) of the people living in poverty around the world are women and girls.

Gender inequality facts

According to statistics produced by Oxfam:
- girls are far less likely than boys to go to school – two-thirds of all children who do not receive an education are girls.
- women earn less than men – women receive 10 per cent of the world's income while working two-thirds of the total working hours in the world.
- women do not have a voice – women are under-represented in governments all around the world.
- women are more likely to suffer violence – the biggest cause of injury and death to women worldwide is violence in the home.

Education, micro-finance, and sport

The case studies in this chapter illustrate how three different charities are tackling three issues. The first shows the importance of education for girls. Studies in sub-Saharan Africa have shown that educating a girl has a huge impact on her future life. She is likely to earn more, and in turn to reinvest that money in her own family. She is likely to have fewer, and healthier, children. Further, in a region with high levels of HIV/AIDS infection, girls who have received an education are three times less likely to catch HIV than uneducated girls.

The second case study is about what happens when you give groups of poor women a chance to run their own small businesses. The third shows what a difference sport can make to the lives of girls in the slums of Kenya.

These women in Rajasthan, India are among those who can be helped by charities that promote equality of education, political representation, and earning power.

Camfed

In 1991, Ann Cotton visited Zimbabwe to investigate why so few girls went to school in rural areas of the country. She found that the main reason was poverty. In sub-Saharan Africa, many families in rural areas cannot afford for their children to go to school. Even if the schooling is free, families often do not have the money to buy uniforms and shoes, or equipment such as pencils and books. If forced to choose, most parents send their sons to school in preference to their daughters because it is commonly believed boys have more future earning power.

Small beginnings

Like many charities, Camfed started small. When Ann returned from her trip to Zimbabwe, she was determined to help some of the girls she had met. She asked her friends and family to help her, and sold baked goods to raise money. Within a couple of years, she was supporting 32 girls through school. In 1993, she founded the Campaign for Female Education – CAMFED.

Camfed's role

The third Millennium Development Goal (see page 10) is "to eliminate gender disparity [difference] in primary and secondary education". Camfed works towards this goal. The charity supports children, mostly girls, in more than 3,000 schools in Ghana, Tanzania, Zimbabwe, Zambia, and Malawi.

At the primary-school level, the charity provides an emergency Safety Net Fund to its partner schools. The money in this fund is used to prevent a child from dropping out of school due to the lack of basic school supplies. However, the costs of high school are considerably higher, and most poor families cannot afford to educate all their children at this level. Once again, it is boys who are usually favoured. But with sponsorship from Camfed, girls can continue through high school, and on to university or to work training programmes. It is crucial to Camfed's work that support for the girls is long-term.

Giving women a voice

*"University education opens many doors.
Not only can women support their families,
they can also influence policies and help
communities in a powerful way."*
*Winnie Farao, supported by Camfed through
high school and college, now working on her
Master's degree*

A vision for the future

Camfed supports individual girls, but it also has an important part
to play in building partnerships with communities and with national
governments. In many cases, women who received their education
through Camfed are now working to make a better future for girls in their
countries. One of these women, Angeline
Murimirwa, was among the first girls to
receive support from Camfed to go to high
school. Today Angeline is the director of
Camfed's Zimbabwe programme.

Students at Mtitu Secondary
School in Tanzania are
supported by Camfed, which
pays their school fees as well
as accommodation and school
uniform costs.

Microloan Foundation

Microfinance is the supply of loans, savings, and other basic financial services to the poor. In practice, many microfinance schemes target women. These financial services often involve only small amounts of money but they can allow poor people to expand their businesses and increase their incomes. The advantage of such schemes is that the people using them are not relying on hand-outs from charities. "Every [dollar] invested in microfinance lives on for the poor long after [it] has been spent," says the Greenshoot Foundation.

How does the Microloan Foundation work?

• *Where?* The Microloan Foundation lends money to groups of 15 to 25 women who want to set up small businesses in sub-Saharan Africa.

• *How does it work?* A typical loan is the equivalent of around $40 (£26) for an individual. Many women who receive loans are living on incomes below the international poverty line of $1.25 per day, so $40 is a lot of money. With the loan also comes eight weeks of training sessions to help women run their businesses. The loan is repaid over four months. Groups meet every two weeks with the local loan officer to repay their loans, and to discuss how they are getting on. Each group member can receive up to four loans, by which time their business should be profitable.

• *What kind of businesses?* Many women set up businesses to buy and sell provisions or food. Some bake bread, make clothes, repair bicycles, or run small tea shops or restaurants.

• *Why only women?* Women tend to have lower-paid work than men and less financial security. Improving the status of women can have a transforming effect on society. Experience has also shown that it is women who feel a responsibility to provide for their children and are keen to succeed in business. As a result, they tend to run their businesses responsibly, make their repayments regularly, and spend the income from their businesses on their families.

A *day in the life*

Chippie is one of the 70 loan officers working for the Microloan Foundation in Malawi. Based in Salima, he travels around his district on a motorbike to make his visits. His job is to collect loan repayments and to train groups of women about managing their money.

7.30 a.m. The day starts with a long bike ride to the first meeting – a repayment meeting. This group have been working with loans from the Foundation for more than four years and have seen their savings and standard of living rise over this time.

10.00 a.m. The second meeting is trickier. Some members of the group cannot make their repayments. But the advantage of working with a group is that other members help out if one or two are struggling.

12.00 p.m. The third meeting is for training. Chippie gives advice about setting up a bank account and managing savings in the long term.

1.00 p.m. Chippie has lunch – fish (from Lake Malawi) and msima (a maize dish).

The afternoon is spent doing paperwork, making sure all the groups' accounts are in order.

Then Chippie returns home for supper and an early night.

This Bangladeshi woman received a microloan from the Grameen Bank for a sewing machine, which she can now use to earn a living.

45

Sport for Social Change

Encouraging young women and girls to play football (soccer) may not at first seem the most obvious way to help them out of poverty. But this is exactly what the charity CARE is doing with its Sport for Social Change Initiative in Kenya.

CARE *and women*

CARE is a US-based charity that started in 1945 to help survivors of World War II. Today, it is one of the leading organizations fighting global poverty. It focuses on working "alongside poor women because, equipped with the proper resources, women have the power to help whole families and entire communities escape poverty..."

Building confidence

CARE believes that sport can have a powerful effect in helping girls to build their confidence and self-esteem. This is especially important for girls who have experienced severe hardships, maybe as a result of natural disaster or conflict, or often because of the effects of HIV/AIDS. Many girls are forced by circumstances to take on heavy responsibilities at a young age – looking after their younger brothers and sisters, for example, or having to find food for their families. CARE believes that playing sport can give them a chance just to be themselves once again.

For the players, football provides a means of escape from daily lives of hardship. Many girls started playing on the streets of the slums where they live, often with homemade footballs made out of plastic bags and string – proper footballs are too expensive.

Creating ambitions

The confidence the girls gain by playing football gives them confidence in other areas of their lives too. The slogan of the campaign, "I am Powerful", says it all. Sport teaches people about teamwork and leadership, about negotiating with others and thinking quickly. All of these skills are vital in everyday life too. Many of the girls in the football team have ambitions for their own lives – to become lawyers or journalists, or to help others like themselves out of poverty.

Kenyan American Soccer Exchange

In 2008, CARE joined with Nike and the Mathare Youth Sports Association to create the Kenyan American Soccer Exchange. A team of Kenyan football players toured several cities in the United States, playing matches against local girls' clubs. For the girls on the Kenyan football team, the trip was a dream come true.

A *great example*

"The KASE team is a shining example of how sport brings young people together to form a strong and united team..."

Maria Bobenrieth, Global Director of Nike's Let Me Play programme

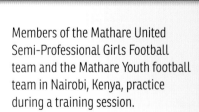

Members of the Mathare United Semi-Professional Girls Football team and the Mathare Youth football team in Nairobi, Kenya, practice during a training session.

TRADE AND DEBT CAMPAIGNS

In 1997, with the approach of a new millennium, a coalition of charities and NGOs came together under the banner "Jubilee 2000". Their aim was the cancellation of the debts that were crippling many LEDCs.

The debt story starts in the 1970s, when many banks in the MEDCs lent money to LEDCs. At that time, **interest rates** (the percentage rates charged for lending the money) were low. But in the 1980s, the interest rates rose. At the same time, the world prices of goods such as tea, coffee, and cotton dropped. Many LEDCs found themselves paying far more for their loans while receiving far less in income from trade in these commodities. Some lenders agreed to "restructure" the loans to allow the LEDCs more time to pay. Others lent yet more money to allow these countries to repay the original loans.

One of the ten concerts held for Live8 in 2005, which called for renewed action against poverty and for debt relief in Africa.

Memories of a campaign

On 16 May 1998, a large demonstration for debt relief was organized by Jubilee 2000. The idea was to surround a meeting of the **G7** (leaders from powerful MEDCs) in Birmingham, UK, with a 9-kilometre- (6-mile-) long human chain. All across the United Kingdom and the world, local volunteers from charities, NGOs, and churches signed up thousands of people to attend the demonstration. Ann Pettifor, Director of Jubilee 2000 at the time, remembers well the highs and lows of that day:

> Just thinking about it makes me shudder. An emotionally charged, positive, uplifting; but also scary day. A roller-coaster of a day. The teams in London and Birmingham consisted of a small core of paid staff; supported by a wide circle of committed volunteers. Both teams started the day exhausted, drained, and fearful. Exhausted by all the hard work; drained by the stress. Afraid that few would turn up. That we would not raise enough money to pay our bills ... That someone would get hurt. Above all, that the massive, collective efforts of thousands of volunteers, would fail to make sufficient impact on powerful, indifferent G7 leaders...

In fact, the G7 leaders did not turn up. The meeting was moved to a different location. Ann continues: "And so it was, that on the day, at 11 a.m. Birmingham was brimming with 70,000 peaceful, cheerful Jubilee 2000 campaigners, their banners and posters. Present also, were about 3,000 journalists, sent to cover the event. Only the G7 leaders were absent..."

A successful action

Yet the day was a success. The wide media coverage of the demonstration persuaded Prime Minister Tony Blair to take notice and he agreed to meet with the leaders of Jubilee 2000.

Heavily Indebted Poor Countries

Campaigns to cancel or reduce the burden of debt on the LEDCs started in the 1980s. In 1996, the World Bank and **International Monetary Fund** agreed a scheme called the Heavily Indebted Poor Countries (HIPC) initiative to reduce the debts of the poorest countries to affordable levels. In 2005, a further initiative was introduced to try to meet the first MDG to tackle extreme poverty. By the end of 2010, the HIPC had resulted in debt packages for 36 countries, 32 of them in Africa. More than $55 billion (£36 billion) of debt has been cancelled under this scheme.

Despite the campaigns and initiatives, many LEDCs continue to spend far more on debt repayment than they do on health care or education. The total debt for all LEDCs stands at $3.7 trillion (£2.4 trillion) – a trillion is 1,000 billion – and in one year they pay out $602 billion (£384 billion) in repayments.

We cannot pay

"The debt cannot be repaid. If we do not pay, our creditors [the lenders] will not die. We can be sure of that. On the other hand, if we pay, it is we who will die. Of that we can be equally sure."

Thomas Sankara, President of Burkina Faso, 1983–1987 (Burkina Faso is one of the HIPC.)

Trade and fair trade

People in the LEDCs grow and make things that people in MEDCs want to buy. Global trade is regulated by the World Trade Organization (WTO), established in 1995. The WTO agrees the rules by which countries trade with each other, but it is dominated by the more powerful MEDCs. This means that the wealthy countries of the world have often made agreements that benefit each other, but which harm the LEDCs. Since 2001, the WTO has been trying to make trade rules fairer but the talks have frequently broken down without agreement.

One highly successful scheme to help producers in poor countries was launched in the 1980s. Fairtrade's mission is to tackle poverty and trade injustice. It works with businesses, communities, and individuals in the LEDCs to improve trading practices and to ensure that farmers and workers can make a sustainable living from what they produce. The first Fairtrade product was coffee, but Fairtrade now includes thousands of food, clothing, and other items – even gold.

Fairtrade sports balls

The Fairtrade label is often associated with small farmers, but it also applies to factory workers. Many factory employees in LEDCs work in terrible conditions, producing goods such as clothes and sporting equipment for sale in the MEDCs. Fairtrade sports balls, including footballs, basketballs, and volley balls, are produced in factories where workers are guaranteed fair wages and conditions. This helps to lift them and their families out of poverty.

These members of the Sahyadri Farmers Consortium, a fair trade organization in Kerala, India, are harvesting organic peppers.

Fair Trade USA

Consumers in the MEDCs have come to trust the Fairtrade label because they believe that it is well regulated and monitored. Fair Trade USA is the leading organization in the United States that certifies fair trade products – it checks that they meet fair trade conditions. It ensures that farmers and workers producing fair trade goods for sale in the United States are paid fair prices and wages, that they work in safe conditions, and that they have the tools, training, and resources for their businesses to thrive.

Who works for Fair Trade USA?

The US operation is based in Oakland, California. Here, people from a wide range of business backgrounds work to connect all the links in the fair trade supply chain – from the producers at one end to the consumers at the other. There are opportunities for volunteer work and for internships, too.

Fair Trade USA: Our Values

"Strong organizations rely on strong individuals. We encourage and support each other to realize our fullest potential, and will thereby strengthen our internal community."

How fair trade makes a difference

Fair trade started with coffee, which has become one of the biggest-selling fair trade products in the world. In Ethiopia, many coffee farmers have organized themselves into co-operatives to sell their coffee on fair trade terms. Some of these groups belong to the Oromia Coffee Farmers Cooperative Union. Founded in 1999, the Union is the largest in Ethiopia, with 34 co-operatives representing nearly 23,000 farmers. The farms are located in Oromia State, in southern and south-west Ethiopia. This region produces about 65 per cent of the country's coffee. It is a mountainous rainforest area where services such as electricity and a clean water supply are rare.

Transforming communities

Fair trade guarantees the farmers a minimum price for their coffee. It also allows them to deal directly with businesses, cutting out the unpredictability of coffee auctions and middlemen. Since 1999, the extra income from coffee sales has helped many communities in Oromia to transform their communities. Recognizing the importance of education in the fight against poverty, Oromia and its members have built more than 15 schools. Oromia has also constructed and staffed several health centres, as well as digging wells to supply clean water in many locations.

A *better price for coffee*

"Fair Trade has definitely helped our community. It has helped us improve our school and water supplies. It has also made a big difference in the guaranteed price we get for our coffee."

Workineh Heldaja, Member of Oromia Coffee Farmers Cooperative Union

Funding a school

"With the extra income from the coffee sales we have built a school and given a dividend to our members who are now able to pay school fees for their children."

Dulecha Gobena, Kilenso Resa Cooperative, southern Ethiopia

Workers in all parts of the Ethiopian coffee industry, including this coffee bean sorter, can benefit when fair trade conditions are met.

JOIN THE FIGHT AGAINST POVERTY

Many of the charities in this book started as a result of the passion and vision of one person or a small group of people. Becoming involved with a charity is one way to make a difference to the world, and there are many different ways you can choose to do this.

Volunteering

Charities need money to run but, just as importantly, they need people's time. You can make a real difference by offering your time to help out with a local charity. Working as a volunteer allows you to make friends with people outside your normal social circle and to feel part of your local community. It could also help you to gain valuable experience and important skills. You can include voluntary work on your CV (curriculum vitae), which will be useful for future college, university, or job applications. Employers always look for "people skills" in potential employees.

The kind of work you end up doing is your choice. Some of the work may be repetitive or hard, but you will be part of a team, and it is good to help people in need.

Here are just a few ideas for volunteering. Note that some of these volunteer positions may be open only to people over a certain age, or in some cases with relevant experience or qualifications:

• in charity offices – some departments need specialist skills, while others just need people with lots of enthusiasm to help out

• in charity shops – sorting donations and staffing the shop

• in warehouses – sorting donated materials for sale in shops or online

• in the community – at fundraising events, or helping needy people

• in food depositories – sorting or handing out food

• at events – volunteers spread the message about the work of a particular charity at festivals or other events by handing out leaflets or working on stalls

• as a speaker – in schools or at events to spread the word about your chosen charity.

Charity shops

One of the first charity shops to open its doors was the Oxfam shop in Oxford in 1948. By 2011, Oxfam had more than 700 shops all over the United Kingdom, selling products donated by supporters and staffed mostly by volunteers. Similar shops raise money for a wide variety of charities all over the world. Most of the stock sold in these shops is second-hand – clothes, toys, and other goods that owners no longer want but which still have plenty of use in them. People usually bring bags of unwanted goods into the shops, and in addition, some charities organize regular house collections. Charity shops are mainly staffed by volunteers, although many charities employ full-time managers to oversee operations in their shops. Volunteers are usually asked to commit to one half-day per week, and they may undertake a range of tasks, including sorting donations, pricing goods, working on the till, and creating window displays.

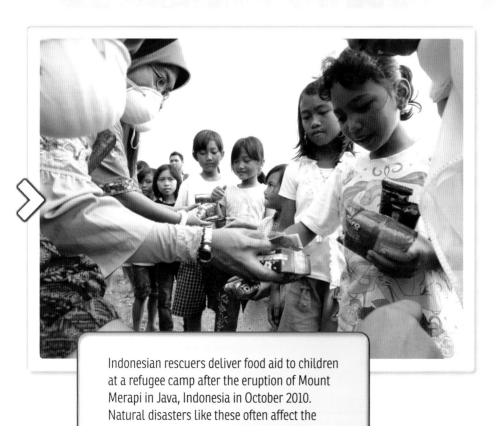

Indonesian rescuers deliver food aid to children at a refugee camp after the eruption of Mount Merapi in Java, Indonesia in October 2010. Natural disasters like these often affect the poorest members of the community most.

Campaigning

In the fight against poverty, campaigning is a vital part of the work that many charities do. Many campaigns succeed because of the weight of public opinion behind them – so your support does count. You can get involved by joining a local group, writing letters, signing petitions, and running stalls at local events to raise awareness of the issues you feel strongly about.

Find out more

If you want to find out more about how you can help in the global campaign against poverty, you could look at these websites:

• End Poverty 2015: www.endpoverty2015.org. Has practical ideas for campaigning against poverty.

• Global Call to Action against Poverty: www.whiteband.org, an alliance of organizations that includes NGOs, women's and youth movements, community groups, and trades unions to call for action from world leaders to meet their promises to end poverty and inequality.

Fundraising

The opportunities for fundraising are endless. At school, you could hold cake sales, no-uniform days, sponsored challenges, or concerts. Charities do their best to make fundraising fun and, most of all, eye-catching – they want people to know about them and to hear their message. For example, Oxfam is encouraging people to organize their own Oxjam music festivals. The charity can help you by providing training days and a complete toolkit of information about how to plan and promote the event. You raise money for Oxfam, learn a lot along the way, and have a great time on the day.

Career choice

If you feel strongly about global poverty and you want to make a difference, one of the best things you can do is work hard at school! There are lots of opportunities for people with good qualifications, experience, and expertise to find paid jobs with charities. For example, just look at the work of Dr Jim Jarvie for Mercy Corps (see page 38)! Many charities offer gap-year opportunities for people between school and university. Others offer internships.

Internships

An internship is a placement, usually unpaid, where young people can learn specific skills while contributing to a charity. Students often take an internship in a field related to the subject they are studying. As an intern, you give your time and skills for free; in return you may gain valuable experience and skills for the future.

Volunteers working for the charity Street Souls hand out food in London. The charity distributes food and sleeping bags to the homeless every few weeks during the winter months.

DEFINITIONS AND STATISTICS

LEDCs and MEDCs

Less economically developed country (LEDC) is a term used by the United Nations to identify the poorest countries in the world. The United Nations looks at various indicators to assess whether or not a country falls into this category. They include:

- average income per person
- nutrition and problems with malnutrition
- health and the under-five mortality (death) rate
- the number of children in education
- the literacy rate – the number of adults who are able to read and write
- the size of the population
- the economy
- the number of homeless people.

In 2011, there were 48 LEDCs:

Africa, 33 countries: Angola, Benin, Burkina Faso, Burundi, Central African Republic, Chad, Comoros, Democratic Republic of Congo, Djibouti, Equatorial Guinea, Eritrea, Ethiopia, Gambia, Guinea, Guinea-Bissau, Lesotho, Liberia, Madagascar, Malawi, Mali, Mauritania, Mozambique, Niger, Rwanda, São Tomé and Príncipe, Senegal, Sierra Leone, Somalia, Sudan, Togo, Uganda, Tanzania, and Zambia

Asia and the Pacific, 14 countries: Afghanistan, Bangladesh, Bhutan, Cambodia, Kiribati, Lao People's Democratic Republic, Myanmar, Nepal, Samoa, Solomon Islands, Timor-Leste, Tuvalu, Vanuatu, and Yemen

Latin America and the Caribbean, 1 country: Haiti

More economically developed country (MEDC) is a term used to describe countries of the world that have highly developed economies. According to Kofi Annan, former Secretary General of the United Nations, "A developed country is one that allows all its citizens to enjoy a free and healthy life in a safe environment." This category covers Europe, North America, Australia, New Zealand, Japan, Singapore, and several Middle Eastern countries.

Millennium Development Goals progress

Target: Halve, between 1990 and 2015, the proportion of people whose income is less than $1.25 a day.

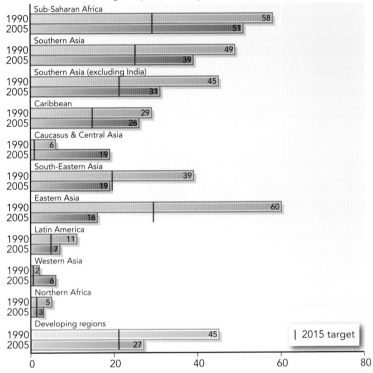

Percentage of people living on less than $1.25 pr day

	1990	2005
Sub-Saharan Africa	58	51
Southern Asia	49	39
Southern Asia (excluding India)	45	31
Caribbean	29	26
Caucasus & Central Asia	6	19
South-Eastern Asia	39	19
Eastern Asia	60	16
Latin America	11	7
Western Asia	2	6
Northern Africa	5	3
Developing regions	45	27

| 2015 target

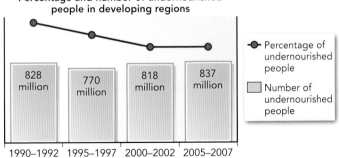

Percentage and number of undernourished people in developing regions

1990–1992	1995–1997	2000–2002	2005–2007
828 million	770 million	818 million	837 million

- Percentage of undernourished people
- Number of undernourished people

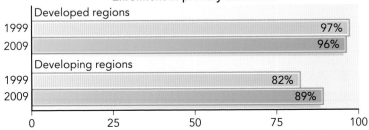

Enrolment in primary education

Developed regions	
1999	97%
2009	96%

Developing regions	
1999	82%
2009	89%

GLOSSARY

absolute poverty describes the state of not being able to afford or have access to the basic essentials for life such as food, shelter, or health care

advocacy activities that allow an individual or a group to have a voice in decision-making that affects them and their lives

cash crop crop that is grown for sale

climate change long-term change in the patterns of weather experienced around the world

counselling advice or guidance to help with a problem, usually from a trained professional

credit in finance, an arrangement where a person buying something does not pay the full amount immediately, but over a longer term

digital divide term used to describe the difference between those who have access to a computer and the internet, and those who do not

donor someone who gives something, for example, money

European Union economic and political union of countries in Europe, established in 1993

fertilize add a substance to the soil to help to make it good for growing crops

G7 group made up of seven major economies in the world: France, Germany, Italy, Japan, the United Kingdom, the United States, and Canada. In 1997, with the addition of Russia, the group became the G8.

gender equality equality between men and women

global warming worldwide rise in the surface temperature of Earth, believed by most experts to be caused by human actions

HIV HIV is a virus that can cause AIDS, an illness that reduces the body's ability to resist infection and which usually results in death if not controlled

humanitarian concerned with the well-being and welfare of people

interest rate in finance, the interest rate on a loan is the percentage rate charged for the use of the money

International Monetary Fund organization founded in 1944 to oversee global financial health and provide assistance as necessary – it has 185 member countries

irrigation supply of water through channels and other devices to help crops to grow

landslide massive ground movement caused by excessive rainfall or other natural events such as earthquakes

less economically developed country (LEDC) see page 58 for full definition

microfinance supply of small loans, savings, and other basic financial services to help individuals or groups start up or run small businesses

Millennium Development Goals (MDGs) the United Nations' Millennium Declaration signed in 2000 by 189 countries worldwide to tackle poverty and its related issues by 2015

more economically developed country (MEDC) see page 58 for full definition

Nobel Prize annual international award given for advances and excellence in the arts and sciences. Nobel Prizes were established by Alfred Nobel, the Swedish chemist who invented dynamite, and first awarded in 1901.

non-governmental organization (NGO) voluntary organization that operates independently from any government, and does not exist to make money

nutrition food that is necessary for health and growth

poverty line measure of the amount of money required for people to be able to afford the essentials, such as food and shelter

relative poverty person in relative poverty cannot afford the items that most people have in their society (for example, in a car or computer in a MEDC)

sanitation services to provide clean drinking water and to remove sewage

sponsorship money given to someone in support of a particular cause

sub-Saharan Africa region of Africa south of the Sahara Desert

sustainable sustainable activities do not damage the environment for future generations

terracing series of flat platforms dug into the side of a hill to allow crops to be grown

World Bank international bank set up in 1944. It is owned by about 180 member countries, and provides financial and technical assistance to LEDCs.

⟩ FIND OUT MORE

Books

Coping With Population Growth (The Environment Challenge), Nicola Barber
   (Raintree, 2011)

Poverty (What If We Do Nothing?), Cath Senker (Franklin Watts, 2011)

Poverty and Economic Issues (Africa Progress and Problems), Tunde Obadina
   (Mason Crest Publishers, 2007)

Poverty and Hunger (Mapping Global Issues), Cath Senker (Franklin Watts, 2011)

Poverty in America: Cause or Effect? (Controversy!), Joan Axelrod-Contrada
   (Benchmark Books, 2009)

Tackling Poverty (Headline Issues), Catherine Chambers (Raintree, 2010)

Suggestions for further research

• Investigate the pros and cons of using celebrities to attract publicity
and funds for charities.

• Find out more about the causes of poverty in the world's MEDCs.

• Investigate why small projects, such as FarmAfrica, are often very effective.

• Find out more about microfinance organizations such as the Grameen Bank
that help some of the poorest people in the world.

• Investigate the everyday products that you can buy under the Fairtrade label.

Websites

General

The Poverty Site: **www.poverty.org.uk/index.htm**
About poverty in the United Kingdom

We Can End Poverty 2015: **www.un.org/millenniumgoals**
United Nations site about the MDGs

World Bank: **web.worldbank.org**
About the World Bank, which provides financial and technical
aid to poor countries

World Poverty: **world-poverty.org/default.aspx**
Looking at the causes of and solutions to world poverty

Campaigning

Global Call to Action Against Poverty: **www.whiteband.org**
An alliance of organizations that call for world leaders to meet
   their promises to end poverty and inequality.

Jubilee Debt Campaign: **www.jubileedebtcampaign.org.uk**
A UK-based campaign to end the debt crisis

One International: **www.one.org/international**
A campaign against extreme poverty

Trade Justice Movement: **www.tjm.org.uk/home.html**
A movement for justice in world trade

Charities

Camfed: **uk.camfed.org**
Helping to educate girls in Africa

CARE: **www.care.org**
International anti-poverty organization

Chicago Food Bank: **www.chicagosfoodbank.org**

e-Learning Foundation: **www.e-learningfoundation.com**
Ensuring children in the United Kingdom have access to computers

UK fair trade movemente: **www.fairtrade.org.uk**

Farm Africa: **www.farmafrica.org.uk**

Goodwill Industries: **www.goodwill.org**
Provides jobs and training for disadvantaged people

MERET/World Food Program: **www.wfp.org/node/14481**
Works with Ethiopian farmers to make farming sustainable

Microloan Foundation: **www.microloanfoundation.org.uk**
Makes small loans to African women

Oxfam: **www.oxfam.org.uk**

Plan International: **plan-international.org**
Sponsors children in poor countries

Send a Cow: **www.sendacow.org.uk**

SOS Children: **www.soschildrensvillages.org.uk**
Runs villages for orphaned children

Venkatraman Memorial Trust: **www.venkattrust.org.uk**
Provides aid for children's education in Kovalam village, Tamil Nadu

War on Want: **www.waronwant.org**

The World Food Program: **usa.wfp.org**

World Vision: **www.worldvision.org.uk**
Runs a child sponsorship programme

INDEX